MW00323954

Ribbons: The Gulf War
A Poem

Books by

WILLIAM HEYEN

Poetry

Depth of Field   (1970)
Noise in the Trees: Poems and a Memoir   (1974)
The Swastika Poems   (1977)
Long Island Light: Poems and a Memoir   (1979)
The City Parables   (1980)
Lord Dragonfly: Five Sequences   (1981)
Erika: Poems of the Holocaust   (1984) (1991)
The Chestnut Rain   (1986)
Brockport, New York: Beginning with "And"   (1988)
Pterodactyl Rose: Poems of Ecology   (1991)
Falling from Heaven: Holocaust Poems of a Jew
    and a Gentile (with Louis Daniel Brodsky)   (1991)

Anthologies

A Profile of Theodore Roethke   (Editor, 1971)
American Poets in 1976   (Editor, 1976)
The Generation of 2000: Contemporary American Poets
    (Editor, 1984)

Fiction

Vic Holyfield and the Class of 1957: A Romance   (1986)

Ribbons: The Gulf War
A Poem

by William Heyen

TIME BEING BOOKS
POETRY IN SIGHT AND SOUND
Saint Louis, Missouri

Time Being Books
10411 Clayton Road
Saint Louis, Missouri 63131

Time Being Books volumes are printed on acid-free paper, and binding materials are chosen for strength and durability.

Library of Congress Catalog Card Number:

ISBN 1-877770-42-2
ISBN 1-877770-45-0 (pbk.)
ISBN 1-877770-47-7 (tape)
ISBN 1-877770-46-9 (tape & pbk. set)

Designed by Ruth A. Dambach
Southeast Missouri State University
Manufactured in the United States of America

First Edition, first printing (November 1991)

The author would like to thank SUNY College at Brockport for a sabbatical during which this poem was written.

Contents

Ribbons: The Gulf War
A Poem

1. (Vegas)

January 14, 1991, hours before deadline in the Persian Gulf.
I've taken my fear to Vegas, coffee & poker,
days minus daylight,

nights minus darkness. I'm at table #1 in the Hilton Flamingo,
facing the wealthy international promenade
past the gold chains

where gawkers gauge our dunes of chips & the lightning deals,
& the rest glide by to shows, roulette,
blackjack, & the big wheel

with one joker among greenbacks that pays 40-1. . . .

Opening a new casino, they hold a ceremony & bury the key
to the front door. I'd like to play forever:
no one's dead here: even Elvis

walked by twice to his gig — he swaggers in white buckskins,
& is thin again. The slots whiz & sing,
reels spinning heterogeneous

misaligned cherries & bars. I'm holding my own in "Texas Hold-Em,"
a grand ahead after four days. Tourists come & go,
I might get eaten yet —

the Flamingo's got a razor beak & deep gullet for such as me. . . .

I keep folding until a pair of paints, or aces, wired, or high cards
close & suited. Last time I slept, I dreamt of soldiers
with slots for brains: they're young,

& smile, & their foreheads revolve with reels
of roses & pterodactyls.
They're there

in the Gulf, my president says, for me, that petroleum-
based vial of shampoo showing up each day
by magic in my room

on the 13th floor. These later hours, I'm often dazed & wondering

→

what I'm doing, & not just here. I'm arrested in the larval,
or gross feeder stage. I know my Thoreau by heart, pal,
while "Desert Shield" progresses

to "Desert Storm." In one hand, a fish paid twice to flop diamonds
to fill his flush to beat my aces & eights. It happens,
& a pro liberated all my chips from him,

in turn, then I nailed her by checking & raising a kings-up boat,
but a missile costs a cool million George Washingtons,
& is fired once, while schools

& soup kitchens go bottoms-up. I signal for a second whiskey

from the cocktail pretty with propped-up tits & high-heeled tail,
a Star Trek Vegan, the evolved pressure of millennia
of animals, insects & lilies. . . .

I check my watch, which might be three hours fast, or slow:
I leave sometime tomorrow, & hope to be home
in my village easy chair

for the great slaughter. Poetry proofs to return to Time Being Books
& *APR* & *Ploughshares* from the semi-trance
of what seems to be

a previous incarnation. I did write one newspaper column early on

in August, a complex of againsts, my only contribution. Anybody
looking for a sullen art ain't seen nothing yet.
I close my eyes to bathe artillery

& tanks in flamingo pink: I've got a pair of bullets that holds up
half the time. I raise to drive speculators out, but
a few stay all the way to the river.

In poetry, the brass screw me, & all the grunts are trigger happy.
Here at the end, it's a double sawbuck to call.
I've been through this before. . . .

I fold, cash in, & set my watch to Brockport & the war.

2. (The Reich)

At first during Vietnam, I didn't know squat.
Wipe the gooks out, I said to my TV set,
which seemed to listen & disgorge body counts.
But I wised up fast, & marched, & wrote, but
nothing much good: naive passion alone.

The best of those poems, maybe, was in *The Nation*,
"Good Money After Bad," about swelling troop deployments
to expand the operation & replace the poor dead bastards
leaving the jungle in body bags. "Coin of the realm,"
I called the drafted victims, & this was mild compared

to the "dogs" & "lumps of dirt" in that manual
& apogee of resistance, the "Essay on Civil Disobedience."
By the long time enough protesters' balls & breasts
clogged the war machine, there were 50,000 names
in the bank for that black marble mirror memorial in D.C.

But I was moving toward the Third Reich by then
by reason of family & reading & ambiguous dreams
in which I ran from Nazis, but with them,
slept in haystacks, but knifed them,
torched a synagogue, but died with Torah in my arms.

3. (Wings)

Dick Hugo once called me about nothing except
to say he'd gotten married, had had a lung cut out,
& would be okay. He was happy & in love & writing.
This was after the White House reception for poets,
where I'd seen him briefly, propped against a baby grand,
blitzed with champagne & history like the rest of us.
Later he wrote me that he'd had to get the hell out,
early — "too many angels there." Jimmy Carter showed up
at the last minute for Rosalynn's receiving line.
My wife & I were next to Simic. When Charlie answered
"New Hampshire," the President's eyes lit up —
the "Live Free or Die" state's primary used to matter —
but then dimmed again with the hostages in Tehran
who would cost him the next election.
Dave Smith, Ashbery, Gwendolyn Brooks, Ammons & Levine,
Stryk, Jim Dickey & Jim Wright, Hall & Swenson &

Rod McKeun was there, who had sold more books
than the other dozens of us together, & William Cohen,
the poetry-writing Senator from Maine; & maybe Gene
McCarthy, whose gnomic *Aardvark* book I'd read —
half Senate jester & one-third politician. Readings, &
Karl Shapiro said something rough & true for the papers,
& we all went home from limbo to decompress
& figure out again what the hell there was to do except
trust to good verses, as royalist Herrick said.
I wish we'd posed on a marble staircase for a photograph:
the angels die off
who for one day visited the powerless residence of power.
I remember being with Han, alone except for the lone
honor-guard Marine standing in shadow in a corner.
One of the smaller rooms, blue or green. Candlelight.
A tall empire bookcase filled with leather wings.

4. (The Peaceable Kingdom)

January 17, 1991. I've walked downstairs in the dark
to watch the war news, but now keep the television shut.

We attacked during the Gulf night. I guess we're screwed
if the jungle of oil under the sand isn't ours,

every orchid & saber-toothed tiger, as long as it lasts —
this is the not-so-secret voice of the stock market. . . .

So, this is how it is to live in a country & to hate.
During this war-to-continue-wars,

I'll hide in these trenches behind barbed wire,
I & Thou, as export armies perform.

What forced my president's warped & oily flame?
I'm either against him, or in bed with him.

5. (The Indian Wars)

I have a boulder out back that I stare at.
Iraq has just hit Israel with six or eight Scuds.
When I'm in power & luck, it's not dark
inside the boulder, but a black silence
edging toward radiance: eternity & nothingness
conjoin for peace. Scuds are cancelled by Patriots,

& vice versa. . . . Back by the boulder I once found
a Seneca arrowhead: this was the western gate
of the five tribes of the Iroquois nation.
In Tel Aviv, gasmasks are packed like lunch.
Inside my television, sparrows whirl in mad patterns
staying alive like yesterday's news which,

as the master of Walden says, is always the same —
a royal wedding reception, or a war somewhere, or a sultan
suffering from gout, or missiles in the weeds like pike.
Another weapon is yclept the "Shrike."
Missiles, like us, have been "thrown into being,"
but ours is the natural tragedy of righteous thinking,

& we are flying 2000 sorties a day into almost no resistance.
"A lot of our old men have become boys again,"
says General Schwarzkopf, Commander of Allied Forces:
for our pilots, there's an element of sandbox fun
to fly in & drop laser-directed ordinance
when there's only one flak-joker in a ten-card deck.

"Schwarz" means black & "Kopf" means head in German.
Germany helped Iraq plan & build their chemical weapons.
Things go round & again go round says Wallace Stevens.
Across Brockport, allegorical ribbons are imposed on trees.
Iraqi television shows the revered warlord on his knees,
praying. He'll keep faith, we'll keep bombing him to heaven.

6. (Sparrows)

A pilot chalks one of his missiles, "For Debra."
She waits there under his wing, a Sparrow.
In Shinkichi Takahashi's eye, sparrows circle

into world without end, without beginning.
Maybe the pilot & his Debra, even before Kitty Hawk,
will some day celebrate Christmas with their four children

in this village where I live in hiding.
I throw seed under a pine for sparrows & mourning doves
who may themselves be Debra in other incarnations. . . .

How many sparrows can we pack under our wings
or set dancing like angels on the head of a pin
before the stars fall, & we lose everything?

7. (Of Palestine)

Technology is working. Laser-guided missiles
round corners & slash into doorways & enter
ventilation shafts of the Iraqi high command.
A Patriot homes in on a Scud, & kills it.

The crisis of poetry reoccurs with each newscast,
how it can't hide forever in impenetrable shelters
under a camouflage of soil & trees. Its heartbeat
falters & slows — is this its hibernation, or burial?
& if the former, when will it awaken & into what
intemperate spring? and if the latter, so be it, amen. . . .

There must be other ways to invoke & praise the oversoul.
I've prayed sixteen prayers on the plants of Palestine
which remains in me, as rapture of aria, & death-knell.

8. (Union)

I've wanted to spiral the path from material
reality to the soul, and you with me.
It could happen unawares, as it probably
must. It could happen with one syllable,
the right sound in the right context,
as it did for Jonathan Edwards who listened
to one word of gospel until transport.

When I was a boy, I once heard God tell me to kneel,
right then & there in the Long Island woods
where I'd been snapping away with my pellet rifle.
The mystics explain union by way of paradox,
"deafening silence," "cold fire," but I,
a boy, knew nothing except leaves as though
my brain & lungs were become leaves. . . .

Time passed, or circled. Later,
a chill & clarity of light, & I was changed,
& lost, & knew. The leaves had fallen, but I'd
nowhere to go, no way to be of them again.

9. (Sorties)

I compare notes with neighbors: never
so many sparrows at our feeders,
thousands waiting out the Brockport winter,
despite hawks. One silhouette didn't shift
when I walked beneath it & slapped its tree,
& last night, quick in the branches of sleep,
leaf-sparrows by thousands teased the predator
to no effect: it digested light in the boughs,
& would. By this time we'd flown 5000 sorties
in the Gulf & had lost only ten planes,
a chance in 500 for each pilot on each mission.
The Iraqi dictator swears to gas Jews, as did
his spiritual mentor, says an Israeli spokesman.
My sparrow understanding scatters at dawn
when a hawk powers through the leaves. . . .

10. (The Word)

I went out into the Brockport woods & vomited.
We are killing Iraqis by the thousands,
burying them with bombs, blowing their limbs off.

Only transcendent poetry is not deluded,
its karma perfect, but no one, today, can write it,
not Whitman, or Rilke, or Rumi, or Mirabai — only God

in God's spacelessness & timelessness says
moment by moment whether any life still lives
in us, the slaughterers, or in our slaughtered.

11. (Mechthild of Magdeburg)

Driving the autobahn from Hannover to Leipzig,
I saw Magdeburg from a distance, & only once.
I remember mists, a gold dome, &, in me, medieval silence.

At twelve, Mechthild of Magdeburg (1210-1297) had a vision,
sensing "all things in God and God in all things."
In Leipzig, soldiers with machine guns

patrolled the streets beneath my skull.
Mechthild's book, *The Flowing Light of the Godhead*, assumes
a mystical oneness of nature & the soul —

not *what* we are, but *that* we are at all is the first miracle —
&, Lord, yes, Your light does travel invisibly in particles
in me, in gold, even in steel gun barrels.

12. (The Circuit)

Readings in Casper, Riverton, Powell, & Gillette
on the Wyoming Poetry Circuit, 1978. Long drives,
sometimes out of range of radio, & missed signals cancelling
one reading somewhere, & snow, & a stuffed bull buffalo
in the Plains Indian Museum, & whiskey at Wild Bill Cody's bar,
& bicentennial pumpjacks rusting the red, white, & blue,
& a missile base in the distance past a herd of antelope,
& a stetson in Shoshone thrown at his girlfriend by a drunk
in peace chains & khakis & an arm prosthesis from the Nam
which now, war in the Gulf a week old, staggers again,
like a season of grief gone by, into every American town.

13. (Conventions)

"This might be an oxymoron," says (I swear) a Pentagon spokesman
beginning to whine, "but why can't we have a civilized war?"
Meaning, I suppose, that when an American airman
bombs your neighborhood, killing maybe a few dozen
& maiming maybe a hundred in body & maybe a thousand in mind,
& he's one of the few planes hit & he has to eject,
& after you've done the best you could to drag
victims out from under debris & you've washed the blood
out of your eyes as best you could & you've captured the bastard,
you should treat him according to the Geneva Conventions,
as gentleman prisoner of war, a name & rank & service number
who deserves a shower & clean clothes. You must not,
as I would, as you would, I swear, if such a technician
killed your wife & children, you must not drive steel
splinters into his eyes until they reach his civilized brain.

14. (Night Vision)

To fill you of the future in –
all's fair in war & prediction –
on Operation Desert Storm:
we bombed the Iraqis, & bombed them,
& bombed them to little opposition,
& were going to keep bombing them
into shocked & dazed submission,
2000 bombing runs a day, & cells
of B-52s (three in triangular pattern),
each bomb blasting a hole 25' deep
by 40' in diameter, & we were grinding
Iraqi bones into powder, were cratering
paths a mile and a half by a mile,
& were flying & bombing by night vision
& were flying noon to noon
& were going to keep bombing when
the Arabs began to call us cowards.
Cowards for not fighting in the sand
where they were dug in like scorpions.
Cowards. & this complex appellation
began to stick: cowards of bombardment
who recoiled from blood unless
it was one general's definition
of the death of thousands of civilians:
"collateral damage in a war." Cowards.
So we began to "engage" them on the ground
& Desert Storm began arriving home, bravely,
as gassed remains in sealed coffins.

15. (Milk)

Last night, the television news receded.
I dreamed myself a meadow surrounded by trees.
Knee-deep in gray grass, I found a key,
& then a door in one of the border trees. At first,
the key was wrong, but then the door opened
& I stood inside myself, at ease. . . .

When I die, I will have no country, except that one.
Will I even know I'm there? —
it will be that peaceful. I won't remember
the destruction of the one plant alleged in all Iraq
to produce infant formula & powdered milk.
I'll feel what a tree at the edge of a meadow feels

in its roots. Leaves are faces there,
but no one I recognize — I won't remember parents,
my wife, my children, or my fears for them.
In that weather, weapons disintegrate
into their elements in the world brain
& can't be thought again.

This is the bark into which word-insects burrow
& lie still for the duration, until
God speaks our incarnation, again,
& we return, as here, in another life, the same one,
maybe, but not. Day after day, the spirit within
feeds on what nothing can ruin.

16. (Occasions)

A new book of poems by an old friend.
One of us is out of touch, probably me.
Today is the twelfth day of the war. Poetry
won't or can't carry national scores,
& probably shouldn't, even if it could.
Eventually, we'll be a metahuman species,
or won't be. At all. In any case,
I do hold in the eye under my breastbone
one of my friend's occasions:
a meadow in England's Lake Country,
a walk among grasses & flowers,
a bird flying a few yards ahead,
seeming to wait, then, like a thought
of the precient summer evening,
flying ahead again. . . . & one day

I was a boy & realized
that all the miraculous light
my hands could hold had streamed
from an origin beyond the sun,
& I'd return. This was the gospel
of the summer field in which I lived
for that little while. Lord, carnage continues
in Your helpless name, & mine.
May the body of the Lake Country somehow
remain in us, visitant from afar,
unmoved by war. In the sounds
of a distant herd winding slowly
o'er the lea. In the vaporous faithfulness
of clouds. In the burst heads
of a hill of daffodils.

17. (The Dead)

Today, the first ground "skirmish," the first American dead.
Names & hometowns will be announced.
Eleven Marines.

I can't imagine them from here, so try to picture just one,
in dress blues, at attention, white gloves,
rifle at his side,

but it's no use. I try to think of eleven, & count
from one to eleven, slowly, & then
try them at rest, then dead,

side by side, on the desert sand, sun in their bronzed faces,
but it's no use. I place them on the floor
in my living room where

they could just fit, but, no, it's no use. On television,
I see our powerful Marines dug in,
helmets pulled low

& gasmasks at the ready, but these are not yet the ones dead,
those whose families will never hold them
in their arms again.

I pass racks in a cargo plane & try to count flag-draped coffins
in the dark drone of transport. No use. I chant
Dulce et decorum est,

pro patria mori, but today stocks shot up fifty points,
& Luciano Pavarotti sang Donizetti
at Lincoln Center

for the Performing Arts. I called my own son & daughter to hear
their living voices, & then took a long walk
out from under news of eleven who,

my president insists, died for me. *Enough*. The dead are myriad
as leaves already forming in the winter boughs.
Enough. I cannot float out-of-body

over our farms or cities to accompany the dead. *Enough.* I cannot
nurse the dead, or feed them, or bury them
in innocent ground.

There will be more dead than there are letters in this lament
& a hundred others. *Enough.* Eleven.
Dead. Unimagined.

January 30, 1991

18. (Politics)

Bartleby's was "the courage not to be,"
says the critic Philip Young, but I am married,
& my wife just phoned. She works for our congressman
who has been informed by the Pentagon that one
of the eleven dead Marines called this district home.
Did I have something, her staff needed to know,
on life or death, some famous quotation
that could possibly comfort, maybe a line
of poetry, something, was there something for a letter
to his parents? . . . I called back later
with my contribution to convention —

In an elegy to a dear friend, America's former
Poet Laureate, Richard Wilbur, wrote: 'Light perpetual
keep him.' We believe that 'light perpetual' will always
keep and hold your dear son in the love and gratitude
of his family and country. Our sincere condolences . . .

— but had meanwhile struck the board & wept,
& had wanted, too, to publish in lights
over Times Square that other Wilbur poem
on the death of Sergeant Tywater in "the good war":
"And what to make of him, God knows.
Such violence. And such repose." . . .

As I write, the body of Marine Lance Corporal
David Snyder, 21, of the 1st Light Armored Infantry Battalion,
begins its long journey home to Kenmore
in the belly of a U.S. cargo plane,
& my congressman's letter to the dead soldier's

stunned & heartbroken parents carries one blossom
of prayerful eloquence: "Light perpetual keep him."

19. (Guesses)

A woman's sweatshirt reads, "Fuck Iraq." I guess
she represents "all that is best in us," as my president says.

In the U.S.A., flags & war toys outsell loaves of bread.
I guess patriotism & violence are our food.

The president declares this Sunday our "National Day of Prayer."
I guess I'll kneel with my church & state under a manhole cover.

A child says, "I hope not a lot of soldiers don't get killed."
I guess not a lot of soldiers haven't not gotten dead.

A leak that seven of the first eleven died by "friendly."
I guess that some die twice, in war & on TV.

We've not yet seen one photograph of one dead American.
I guess they are sanitized & reassembled under the Pentagon.

One of our missiles is called the "Tomahawk."
I guess we're using primitive weapons to scalp Iraq.

Between bombing reports, commercials for lingerie & body lotion.
I guess, as the president says, "life must go on."

B-52s' special "penetration bombs" shudder underground.
I guess the desert has become our sexual field.

America — "the finest, most loving nation on earth."
I guess at the president's meaning, & brush my teeth.

Ironic that irony is not my mode.
I guess, like the Gulf, I need my mouth washed out with crude.

I guess I'm a victim of "modest collateral damage."
I guess I'll have my bible bound in camouflage.

20. (Action)

During the fourth day of the Warsaw "Aktion," July 25, 1942,
a group of Jewish policemen & civilian helpers were rounding up
scores of victims for deportation to the dreaded East,
Treblinka. They'd formed a ring of truncheons around captives
& beat those who tried to push out.
Down the block, two lorries waited, two Nazi soldiers
leaning against them. Witness Janina Bauman says,
"they watched the round-up lazily, talking and laughing
in the bright sunshine of the mid-summer day."

During the third week of the Gulf War, February, 1991,
I pay my taxes & watch the news I've paid for.
The Warsaw "Aktion" took place from 8-4 daily,
but CNN is round-the-clock & our bombers have night vision.
Thousands of citizens were driven to the *Umschlagplatz*
for torahtrain passage to Jewish heaven.
Leaning back in my Brockport easy chair,
I am lazy with decaf & waiting for my money's worth,
maybe a tank battle, or fuel-bomb suicide mission.

21. (Rx)

Relief to visit this enormous tonnage of ordinance
on our enemy. Continued *relief* as long as our intelligence
"acquires" what a pilot calls a single "lucrative target."
What else could we have done with it,

this weaponry crushing our brains in their coral reefs,
our hearts in their caverns of salt? Almost rheumatic
with lung-missiles. Clusters of bombs in our kidneys.
Now, *relief.* Physiological. Cathartic.

22. (The Chair)

Will there be, & when, a ground war? —
"The $64,000 Question." . . . In that '50s game show,
placed in an isolated box like death-row prisoners
to ponder a six-part brain-buster on military history, maybe,
or Shakespeare, some contestants had been fed the answers,
but screwed their brows into fake pain, & grimaced.
We looked into the window of their isolation chamber
& rooted for such specialist brilliance to prevail.
Several won fame, & bail, & suspended sentence.

Now someone knows that big dough's on the line
& bored districts needing some patriotic dead,
& arms contracts. More softening from the technological air
before gasmask-to-gasmask stuff. My easy chair's adjustable
for the long wait, or short. My "coalition forces"
will destroy Kuwait & then invade to free it.
Iraq's planted a mine every six feet on every channel.
Hate to admit it, but the Super Bowl's over, Buffalo lost,
& we here in New York's Wild West would welcome some blood.

23. (Home)

On the tenth of December, 1971,
I stepped outside the visitors' building at Bergen-Belsen
to walk among the mass graves. Overhead,
an occasional crow gusted across the overcast;
on the graves, restless low erika parted & flattened
with streaks of wind, then
recomposed. That night I drafted

a memoir that carried an epigraph by Peter Weiss who said
that only one place, where he had spent
only one day — Auschwitz — stood firm
in the topography of his life.
At Belsen, underfoot, after so much flesh
melted away, the historical solidity
of bones. I was born in 1940

in America, have spent much of my life in only
two places, & in poetry,
but since that one afternoon have yearned, as you have, for a home
beyond this one, this cave
now so smoke-choked with greed & hate
that we won't be able, for long,
to live in it.

24. (The Frog)

Lao-Tzu says, "Compassionate toward yourself, you reconcile
all beings in the world." Kuwait's oil wells
are all "deep-mined," we're told,

&, if set afire, could darken a few growing seasons around
our delicately-calibrated earth.
Iraq & its "19th province"

provide a research lab for our new "smart weapons,"
& the Pentagon's procurement cup
runneth over, but

because my own brain is bleeding missiles & meadowlarks,
I'm draining a bloodbank of ecstatic poems:
Ghalib declares,

"The world is no more than the Beloved's single face;
In the desire of the One to know its own beauty,
we exist." A perfect circle back

to Emerson's Oversoul: thus, murder is suicide, we bomb ourselves,
& all in a desperate heart-doomed prayer for Oneness
& home. This is the sound of the frog

that leapt into Basho's pond & disappeared, but its green face
surfaces, & winks, in my own coffee cup. I taste
the Tigris & Euphrates in every sip.

25. (The Parrot)

In the middle of this fourth week of the war,
pilots of the allied coalition forces all insist
they are doing their best, even at increased personal risk,
not to bomb civilians, & I believe them. But,
still, we're killing about 50-100 a day,
& some of the disfigured & orphaned may be worse off.

My mind clears like a cloudless morning in the desert.
One palm, & in this palm a parrot, gaudy & loud.
As the sun continues its trajectory toward noon,
the parrot screams. Some pilots can hear it,
or will, before war's end, which will never end for them.
I can't stand, who can, that screaming, & for how long?

26. (Soul)

26th day of the war, a Monday, snowing heavily in Brockport
& proverbially cold. On Wall Street the bulls stampede.
I realize once & for all that money doesn't care if the world
perishes as long as its last fix is profit. Entwined
with bombing runs, oil lanes flow the red that's green,
& the Iraqi dictator has just drafted all his 17-year-olds,
& in a Yale cellar my president renews his pledge to Skull & Bones,
but, as the guest on a talk-show argued, "in the '90s, people
should be less opinionated," so getting along might mean
how not to mention the world's oceans going dead & forests
converted to chopsticks & consumer brains blitzed by maxi-malls
on shopping channels selling birthstone doorstops & baseballs signed
by heavy-hitting criminals & politicians; how not to notice the oil

six feet deep & deepening in that gulf between the new cerebral cortex
& the old medulla oblongata. I remember how in grammar school
we learned the cycles of reptiles & trees & the symmetry of snowflakes
as part of the great mystery of our natural lives.
We were "planetary beings," my 6th-grade teacher said.
We lived on a star & were drifting toward heaven, for all we knew,
but now 65,000 misguided (pardon) sorties of the coalition allied
against ourselves, & the miracle of tiny frozen hexagons
falling by billions around my village home,
one for each person who ever lived, a snowstorm meditation
& hieroglyph from God. In my humble opinion,
each flake is charged with a particle of soul. Near the end,
only one thing matters, & it's not for spoils, or for sale.

27. (Ribbons)

Across America
        ribbons & bows
              vote in our trees

    but for what
        enlist our trees
            but into what

    debate our trees
        weep in our trees
           pledge

allegiance in our trees
        but to what
          lobby in our trees

 confuse our trees
        patronize our trees
           transfix our trees

    but for what
        testify in our trees
          twist & rot

    into what
        fade from our trees
          into what

28. (Ordinance)

Here in Brockport it's Main & State.
In every village or town or city,
one intersection thought of as central, inseparable
from consciousness of place. & that's the place,
be it resolved, in every village or town or city,

that two KIAs should be laid out
on wooden biers in the street, one American & one Iraqi,
side by side, hand in hand among the blowing leaves
& headlines, until uniforms have rotted away
& the dead shine like white shards, our traffic

bending around them, the war brought home
by this memorial, weather & bone, where we abide
in history, in the human ribbon of time, & folly,
& sacrifice. But it's no use: children in their buses
will stop pointing, & we won't notice when

the skeletons' ribcages cave in, & someone
at a schoolboard meeting or in city council will say
we ought to clear those skulls & stuff away,
from every village or town or city,
whatever all that stuff is, resolved, & we do.

29. (Gifts)

First day of the fifth week of the war.
"Desert Storm" there, winter storm here.
In Iraq, the removal of bodies & body parts
& fused lumps of unidentifiable remains
from what we call a command bunker
& what they call a civilian bomb shelter

& which was one or the other, or both.
In Brockport, snow outlines pastel ribbons
in my neighbors' trees along our streets
cleared by nightshift plows, & sanded
as we slept. In Baghdad, women in black
search & mourn among the blanketed dead

dragged out of their devastated haven.
Air raid sirens are still keening
while here the snow softens everything
in the fallen world. A White House spokesman
informs us that human life hasn't the "sanctity"
for their president that it does for mine,

& I don't want to live, sometimes — do you?
The blankets are not khaki, but civilian,
in rich colors & sacred Islamic designs.
All day across this country we'll open
cards & heart-shaped boxes of candy.
Happy Saint Valentine's.

30. (Northward)

1.

A missile is of course a penis, & war
turns us on,
& some condoms shine in the dark like tracers, & war
turns us on,
& thousands of women choose breast flag-tattoos, & flags
turn us on,
& someone markets yellow & orange ribbon panties, & ribbons
turn us on,
& flags coming to the tops of flagpoles, & arsenals
turn us on,
& the *Schadenfreude* & solemn pomp of military funerals
turn us on —
I won't admit it, I'll look away, I won't tell.

2.

No need to fill you of the future in — the war
did not/does not end,
but over Brockport these last February days,
V's of geese
wavering their way northward, never, in my remembrance,
so early.
Even when I sleep, the almost unintelligible
wingbeats
from far & near somewhere. My sour mouth
after vomit
sweetens with a mystery of water
drawn up
from under the temporal desert.

31. (Praise)

A lull in my attention. On day 34 of the Gulf War,
it's almost 50° in Brockport. A month more of winter,
& the first male redwings will whistle in wetland cattails.
In my backyard, the half century-old silver maple swells
toward buds & leaves stored in its memory cells,

& there will come a morning when I wake outside
my winter skull, but not yet, but, still, the war dead
& dead-to-come, today, recede. Arabia is fabled
& far away as a pyramid in an N.C. Wyeth oil
in a Scribner's Classic. Iraqi withdrawal

hinges on a Russian peace initiative flying at eve
to Washington & Baghdad. If it's shot down, our massive
amphibious-air-ground assault begins. In Amherst,
an unknown civilian soaked his clothes with paint thinners
& set himself on peaceful fire. Like Buddhist monks in Nam

in their robes of yellow & orange & sparrow flame.
Today, I notice the green tips of daffodils
poking up through melting snow, & fathom
undiminished praise in the calls of mourning doves,
undiminished praise in the calls of mourning doves.

32. (Roses)

Day 37. What's going on? As I do in mine,
the whole country sits back in its television chair
as negotiations & the war progress. Confusion
of doves & hawks, the Russians & Iraq,
my president due to demand & doublespeak

in the Rose Garden. The Pentagon's invasion
can't jack up, can't come, *now*, can it?
A soldier says that the whole situation's
like "a barrel of eels in spit."
We've got 37 diplomats at every airport. . . .

He steps out into balmy Washington sunshine
& delivers an ultimatum. Noon tomorrow,
unless, or else. The roses show
no color yet, but their intelligence, secret
to us still, knows we'll always be at war

somewhere, genes & history in no hurry,
I suppose. A "soft target" is when
you're hitting more troops than hardware.
I admire the multiple launch rocket system
which blooms with chromosomes, our only poetry.

33. (Mastodon)

The bones of the largest prehistoric woolly-haired mastodon
ever found in North America lay in blue clay
at the bottom of a deep hole
under the murky, smoke-filled Aucilla River in North Florida.

The divers' underwater lamps first
picked out the animal's lower jaw, then a pile of long leg bones.

This was 1968 when
Johnson could not run again &, in Chicago,
at the Democratic National Convention, heroic protest crippled
our berserk war machine.

The animal once measured about 11' at the shoulder.
One of its tusks is 9'6", the other is broken

off about 1'6" shorter.

34. (Its Hour Come Round)

I've twice heard a general use the word "ripple,"
"a ripple of bombs." Half my childhood
at ponds. A ripple of bombs.

& the phrase "preparing the battlefield," as, each spring,
we till our gardens & prepare the soil
for tomatoes & vegetables.

A ripple across the evolving battlefield of the mind,
some enormous creature engorged
with bark & blood

slobbers toward us, still ravenous, from the sacred cave
where words are first sounded & shaped,
where it has fed,

& I'm afraid of & for all the boys & girls in my neighborhood
marching with lollipops & machine guns
among the ribbons.

35. (The Heart)

One mid-century Long Island afternoon
I biked over for some schoolyard basketball.
My older brother Werner & his friends, that melting-pot gang:
Tony Routi, the Blumbergs, Ernie Olsen, Prez, Riley & the rest.
Later, they were just hanging around, smoking, telling dirty jokes,
when one of them — I've blocked out who — mentioned a movie
playing in Smithtown, a war movie. He said you saw
a Japanese soldier cut the heart out of an American prisoner.
He said the prisoner was still alive, & tied to a stake,
& the Jap had a razor-sharp sword, & cut the heart right out
of the prisoner's chest, right through bone, & held it in his hands.

I am fifty now & have heard, I guess, almost everything.
I have read Krafft-Ebing, true stories of genitals in soup,
& have followed serial murders on television, have witnessed
secondhand such lurid torture & dismemberment
that I am almost shock- and compassion-immune. I have seen
an American president's head blown apart, bits
of his brain & skull sticking to his wife's pink skirt,
& have been to Bergen-Belsen where Anne Frank died.
But I was only ten that afternoon when
for the first time in my mind a human body was cut open,

its heart removed, & I could not breathe well or sleep well
for a long time, & this morning, watching television news,
I heard a young political science major, one Randall Alden,
being interviewed at the University of California at Irvine
about this war in the Gulf, which he was for 100 percent,
& if it were not concluded very soon, he urged bombing civilians
& deployment of U.S. tactical nuclear weapons, & for him
the Iraqi people were not people, & our oil economy
was his religion, & I lost hope, for I knew, then, what had become
of the American whose heart had been cut out.

36. (The Ruby)

The talk-show host keeps saying "Thanks for calling"
& tries not to blink beneath his mask. It ain't easy:
the guy from Cleveland called all reporters Nazis;
Los Angeles said America should apologize & retreat;
Miami blamed everything on "spit-curled" Hassids in Tel Aviv.

As Kabir says, everyone is searching for the great ruby
which — despite our military's "adequate terrain assessment" —
can't be found in the oceans, or under rocks, or sand,
or anywhere in the East, or West, but only in the stars
under the breastbone where it's impossible to see except

with your third eye turned inward. Sort of obscure
down there among arteries & rib-trees. I feel
for the glimmery blood-red gemstone in depths of protoplasm,
the basis of the living universe, & can't grasp it, yet,
but still sense that it's down there somewhere.

37. (Reasons)

In my American home, a walk-in closet. . . .
Behind furs & barrels of oil, a door. . . .
Stairs winding downward for years
as I descend, in hiding, to somewhere beneath
martial music & parades to the cynical truth:

my dolphin, cormorant, dragonfly eye darkens:
I've made the world safe again for the war machine
guarding the fossil fuel pipeline between the old brain
& the new, have freed vast ancient jungles
beneath the sand so I can buy & burn them. Therefore,

the dead did not die in vain: two to three hundred Americans,
a thousand times that many Iraqi enemies & future
business partners done in objectively by 110,000 "surgically clean"
bombing missions of the coalition forces allied against
any eastern takeover of our battle for extinction.

38. (The Truth)

Across Brockport Village, a blight of orange & yellow ribbons
meant to remember our half-million participants
in "Operation Desert Storm," those who put their lives on line
to protect our country, as our president says.
Darkening ribbons encircle trees, telephone poles,
mailboxes, porch rails — so I was understandably half bored
& half nuts with war & ugliness, so climbed to my roof
& tied a large black configuration of bow & ribbons
to my aerial. Up there, I saw how it divides the winter sky
with its alphabet of one emotional letter, a vowel. . . .

At first, no one noticed, but then a car turned around.
Later, a police cruiser slowed down, & then another.
A reporter stopped for that infamous photo that appeared in *Time*
& the first of a hundred interviews I declined,
& neighbors gathered. My phone kept ringing off the wall,
people yelling "bastard," & "traitor," & "get it the hell down,
or else." . . . Eventually, my best friend came to my door
& asked me why. I explained, "I can't explain." Others followed,
& insisted. "No comment," I said. "I don't want trouble,"
I said. "Read Hawthorne's 'The Minister's Black Veil.'"

I still like the way the black bow & ribbons flutter,
stark but suggestive of comic dark, serious, direct,
my own American allegiance & patriotic light.
Parson Hooper had his reasons, & half understood them,
but when he slept or spoke, his breath trembled the veil,
& even holy scripture seemed filtered by the terrible
transformation of black crepe into symbol. In the end,
not even his creator could commend the visionary parson
who espied the truth that separates & condemns.
Above my village, this beauty of black bow & ribbons.

39. (The Job)

1.

In March of 1968 when Charlie Company at last withdrew
from the village of My Lai where,
casually brutal, they'd tortured, raped, slaughtered, buried
innocent unarmed civilians by the dozens —

after they withdrew, Lieutenant William Calley & the rest,
they spent that night, & we with them in spirit,
in a Vietnamese graveyard, our sleeping bags & weapons strewn,
then & now, amidst stone lanterns & shrines.

2.

In March of 1991 after our elite technicians left off
incinerating defenseless fleeing defeated
Iraqi enemy & banked away from thousands of meat fires,
the charred & gaping human forms grilled out

along a 60-mile corridor north of Kuwait City, we at home gathered
to sing "God Bless America" & the questioning
"Star Spangled Banner" & prayed thanks that we'd gotten the job done,
whatever it was, we try to remember, poppies & ribbons.

40. (Storm Coda)

1.

March 4, 1991: arrived at midnight, an ice storm,
worst weather here, or anywhere else I've ever lived,
of the century. Woke in the dark to thunder
of trees cracking around me. Brockport without power
today & for days to come. I'll be fortunate
if the great elm beside our garage holds firm
under the weight of the next 24-48 hours
of freezing rain & sleet. I walked out twice

to one open place at a crossroads & heard what
seemed like cannon shots across the treed lots,
& emergency chain saws from all directions.
The cold deepens, & the dangerous thickness of crystal
& diamond. In my yard, I scattered fifty pounds of seed
while mourning doves, a pair of cardinals, juncos, sparrows
darted in by hundreds among the fallen & falling limbs.
Where & how did any survive the night, I wondered. . . .

2.

Today or yesterday, under a tent somewhere
in the sand, occurs/occurred the ceremony
of surrender. Here, apple pie & a thermos
of blowtorch coffee with neighbors for company.
Later, kool-aid & cold spaghetti & the oblivious
imposition of hawk-talk going in one ear
& catching in my brain like an arm hung up
on a branch over a sparking wire. Just before

ceasefire, thousands more Iraqi dead,
the last killed when our dutiful technicians
cluster-bombed flocks of defenseless tanks,
bikes, luxury cars & carts fleeing north from
karmic revenge for their own tortured & murdered victims.
Here, ribbons coated with inch-thick ice,
or blasted or tangled in fallen trunks & limbs,
or stripped bare from trees in explosive cascades,

3.

or impaled, or buried. I've constructed this coda
by the light of a cedar-scented candle.
Over my village, a ribbon of siren wavers in nightwind.

41. (Epilogue)

1.

From its crowded clump in the wood, I transplanted
a six-foot cherry sapling beginning to bud.

I'd meant well for it, had pruned its branch-tips,
had dug it an ample ball, had lugged it in wet burlap

to my ice-freshened field, had tamped it
into a deep loam bed, had staked it, watered it,

circled it in my hands several times for a long time,
had blessed it — or at least prayed thoughts for it to blossom

from our warming Brockport winters for a century or more —
& then stood off a ways, smug with ideas of oxygen & nurture

here on this acre meant to balance the depletions of my own life.
But the tree never took. I waited weeks, a month, three,

sliced my thumbnail into twigs drying out despite
sequences of showers & all hosannahs of spring sunlight. . . .

2.

That was the year of our first war in the desert
from which we returned to amnesiac parades

in our marble capital & under tickertape blizzards
in the canyons of New York: while dozers still censored

hapless Iraqi fodder across those burning lands:
while a half-million children would yet perish

as a direct result of American intelligence & skill
& relentless play. O Father in your Xian heaven,

when did we not mean even to mean well, if not then? . . .
That was the year of our hundred-day slaughter

when spring, with no reason, in Your inexorable wisdom
just the same, despite the single harbinger

of my dead sapling, deployed itself again, transcendent,
to fuel my fossil heart, & You did nothing to stop it.

WILLIAM HEYEN

William Heyen's poems have appeared in more than a hundred periodicals, including *The New Yorker, Harper's, TriQuarterly, Poetry,* and *American Poetry Review.* His honors include two fellowships from the National Endowment for the Arts, the John Simon Guggenheim Fellowship in Poetry, the Eunice Tietjens Memorial Prize from *Poetry* magazine, and the Witter Bynner Prize for Poetry from the American Academy and Institute of Arts and Letters. Mr. Heyen's previous books include *Depth of Field, Long Island Light, Erika: Poems of the Holocaust, Lord Dragonfly,* and *The Chestnut Rain.* His next two volumes of poetry, *Pterodactyl Rose: Poems of Ecology* and *The Host: Selected Poems, 1965-1990,* as well as *The Green Gate: Essays on Poetry and Ecology,* are forthcoming from his publisher, Time Being Books of St. Louis, Missouri. Mr. Heyen is currently Professor of English and Poet in Residence at the State University of New York College at Brockport.

Also available from **Time Being Books**

LOUIS DANIEL BRODSKY
You Can't Go Back, Exactly
The Thorough Earth
Four and Twenty Blackbirds Soaring
Mississippi Vistas: Volume One of *A Mississippi Trilogy*
Forever, for Now: Poems for a Later Love
Mistress Mississippi: Volume Three of *A Mississippi Trilogy*
A Gleam in the Eye: Poems for a First Baby

WILLIAM HEYEN
Pterodactyl Rose: Poems of Ecology
Erika: Poems of the Holocaust

LOUIS DANIEL BRODSKY and WILLIAM HEYEN
Falling from Heaven: Holocaust Poems of a Jew and a Gentile

Please call or write for a free catalog.

TIME BEING BOOKS
POETRY IN SIGHT AND SOUND
Saint Louis, Missouri

10411 Clayton Road • Suites 201-203
St. Louis, Missouri 63131
(314) 432-1771

TO ORDER TOLL-FREE
(800) 331-6605 Monday through Friday, 8 a.m. to 4 p.m. Central time
FAX: (314) 432-7939